Marc-Antoine Charpentier

Pestis Mediolanensis
(The Plague of Milan)

Early Musical Masterworks—Critical Editions and Commentaries

GENERAL EDITORS
Howard E. Smither
Vincent Duckles
Charles Hamm

Orazio Vecchi's "L'Amfiparnaso,"
edited by Cecil Adkins

Josquin des Prez's "Missa Pange lingua,"
edited by Thomas Warburton

Marc-Antoine Charpentier's "Pestis Mediolanensis"
edited by H. Wiley Hitchcock

Marc-Antoine Charpentier

Pestis Mediolanensis
(The Plague of Milan)

Dramatic Motet for
Soloists, Double Chorus,
Woodwinds, Strings, and Continuo

Edited by

H. Wiley Hitchcock

The University of North Carolina Press · Chapel Hill

Cut on title page: Prelude to *Pestis Mediolanensis* (Paris, Bibliothèque Nationale, Ms. Rés. Vm¹ 259, vol. XVII, fol. 41ᵛᵒ).

Grateful acknowledgment is made to the Bibliothèque Nationale, Paris, for permission to reproduce pages of the manuscript of *Pestis Mediolanensis*, and to M. François Lesure, Conservateur-en-chef of the Département de la Musique, for assistance in obtaining photographs of them.

Music autography by
Helen M. Jenner

© *1979 The University of North Carolina Press*
All rights reserved
Manufactured in the United States of America
ISBN 0-8078-1365-6
Library of Congress Catalog Card Number 79-320

Library of Congress Cataloging in Publication Data

Charpentier, Marc-Antoine, d. 1704.
 [Pestis Mediolanensis]
 Pestis Mediolanensis—The plague of Milan: dramatic motet for soloists, double chorus, woodwinds, strings, and continuo.

 (Early musical masterworks)
 1. Oratorios—Scores. I. Hitchcock, Hugh Wiley, 1923– II. Title. III. Title: The plague of Milan. IV. Series.
 M2000.C5P5   782.8'2'54   79-320
 ISBN 0-8078-1365-6

Contents

Charpentier: A Biographical Sketch 3

Notes on *Pestis Mediolanensis* 5
  General Background 5
  Source and Dating 5
  The Text 6
  The Music 6

The Present Edition 8
  Performing Forces 8
  Time-Signatures and Tempos 11
  Other Editorial Commentary 11
  Previous Edition; Phonorecording 12

Text of *Pestis Mediolanensis* 13

Score of *Pestis Mediolanensis* 15

Readings 64

Index 73

Marc-Antoine Charpentier

Pestis Mediolanensis

(The Plague of Milan)

Charpentier: A Biographical Sketch

The birthdate of Marc-Antoine Charpentier is unknown. The date most often given, 1634, derives from Titon du Tillet, who in his *Description du Parnasse françois* (1727) says that Charpentier died "in the month of March 1702 at 68 years of age." But Titon du Tillet has the date of death wrong: it was 24 February 1704, as we know from the records of the Sainte-Chapelle du Palais in Paris, of which Charpentier was *maître de musique* when he died. And 1634—or even 1636—as the year of the composer's birth seems too early in any case, for stylistic and other reasons. Circumstantial evidence suggests a time between 1662 and 1667 for Charpentier's years of study with Carissimi in Rome. If, as Titon du Tillet and others even closer to Charpentier (such as Sébastien de Brossard) say, he was "in his youth" at the time (confirming the poet-musician Dassoucy, who speaks of Charpentier as a "garçon" in 1672), an estimated date of birth no earlier than 1645–50 is perhaps close to the mark.

Charpentier's study with Carissimi was of several years' duration—three, according to the *Mercure galant* of February 1681. His earliest music offers ample evidence of his absorption of mid-century Italian musical style, and among his extant holographs are copies of Carissimi's oratorio *Jephte* and the *Missa Mirabiles elationes maris* for four choirs by Francesco Berretta.

We are not certain in what capacity and by whom Charpentier was first employed when he returned to Paris from Rome. Some have said—again, basing the claim on Titon du Tillet's account—that he was employed immediately by Marie de Lorraine, Duchesse de Guise (1615–1688), who boasted one of the largest private musical establishments in France, at least after she inherited her family's fortune in 1675 and moved into the Hôtel de Guise in the Marais district of the city. But internal evidence among the hundreds of musical manuscripts by Charpentier that have been preserved suggests that he was employed as a composer by her only during the period from about 1683 until her death. Long before that, he had been associated with the troupe of Molière (known after 1680 as the Comédie-Française).

In 1672 the collaboration between Molière and Jean-Baptiste Lully had collapsed upon the latter's entrance, with monopolistic royal privileges, into the field of opera composition and production. Molière thereupon approached Charpentier to write music for his plays. When *La Comtesse d'Escarbagnas*, which had received its premiere performance at the court of Louis XIV on 2 December 1671, was first played before the public in Paris (8 July 1672), it had an overture by Charpentier, and, instead of preceding the *Ballet des ballets* with Lully's music (as it had the previous December), it preceded a revival of *Le mariage forcé* with new entr'acte *intermèdes* by Charpentier. The association between the composer and the Comédie-Française was to be a long one, lasting until 1686, although Molière's death during the first run of *Le malade imaginaire* in 1673 had put an early end to his personal collaboration with Charpentier.

By the early 1680s Charpentier was in the employ of Monseigneur, the Grand Dauphin, and was for a time his musical director, composing for him both secular stage works and chapel compositions. In 1683 the composer presented himself as a candidate for one of the four newly created positions of *sous-maître* (i.e., composer) of the King's chapel, but illness prevented him from appearing for the second of two eliminations among the various candidates. A scant two months later, Louis XIV granted him an annual pension, perhaps as a consolation prize or else in gratitude for his service to the Dauphin. This was as close as Charpentier came to enjoying royal patronage, although later he again approached the edge of the court circle when he became music teacher to Philippe, Duc de Chartres (later to become Duke of Orléans and then Regent of France).

Also in the 1680s, Charpentier was employed, as we have seen, by the Duchesse de Guise, both as singer (he was an *haute-contre*—a high tenor) and as *maître de musique* and composer. For the de Guise establishment he wrote some eight stage works (including a reworking, under the title *La couronne de fleurs*, of his setting of the original prologue of Molière's *Le malade imaginaire*), a number of motets, psalm settings, and oratorios, and an *Idyle sur le retour de la santé du Roi*.

In the same decade, and perhaps earlier, Charpentier was associated with the principal church of the Jesuits in Paris—Saint-Louis (later renamed Saint-Paul-Saint-Louis), in rue Saint-Antoine— which made him *maître de musique* and for which he composed a large number of sacred works. Brossard speaks of the position as being "among the most brilliant" in French musical life. Le Cerf de la Viéville termed the Jesuit church "l'église de l'opéra," and in fact some of Charpentier's manuscripts of sacred works from this period include the names of well-known singers at the Opéra. Besides writing for the church of Saint-Louis, Charpentier also contributed to the sacred dramas of Jesuit colleges like the Collège d'Harcourt (*Ouverture du prologue de Polieucte*) and the Collège Louis-le-grand (*Celse Martyr*, 1687; *David et Jonathas*, 1688), as well as to a number of convents and abbeys (Port-Royal, l'Abbaye aux Bois).

After Lully died in 1687, other composers could finally write *tragédies lyriques* for the Opéra. Charpentier composed one, *Médée*, to a libretto by Thomas Corneille, that was first produced on 4 December 1693, but it was not a great success (for musico-political reasons, according to Brossard).

On 20 May 1698 the post of *maître de musique* of the Sainte-Chapelle fell vacant with the death of the incumbent, François Chaperon. A month later Charpentier was named to the job, which he held until his own death. It was a prestigious position, second in French sacred music only to the directorship of the royal chapel at Versailles. Some of Charpentier's richest and most impressive music was composed for the Sainte-Chapelle during these six years, including a giant *Motet pour une longue offrande* and the dramatic motet *Judicium Salomonis* (both written for the annual "Messe rouge" of the Parlement, the chief French judicial body, which was celebrated in the Sainte-Chapelle); massive settings of Psalms 70, 26, and 15; and the masterpiece among his Masses, *Assumpta est Maria: Missa 6 vocibus cum symphonia*.

Practically none of Charpentier's music was published during his lifetime, only some entr'acte airs for the play *Circé* (1676), a full score of *Médée* (1694), and a number of brief *airs sérieux et à boire* (appearing mainly in various issues of the *Mercure galant*). A few years after his death, twelve of his smaller motets were published by his nephew and inheritor Jacques Edouard (*Motets mêlez de symphonie*, 1709); other slight works appeared posthumously in the annual volumes of *Meslanges de musique* issued by the firm of Ballard. Fortunately, the bulk of Charpentier's manuscripts was kept intact by his legatee Edouard and sold by him to the King's library in 1727; bound in twenty-eight massive volumes, this collection of "Mélanges autographes" is now in the Bibliothèque Nationale in Paris. Together with a few other manuscripts including music by Charpentier (notably a group collected by Brossard, these also now in the Bibliothèque Nationale), the extant works by the composer number more than 550. This considerable legacy may be summarized as follows:

Sacred vocal works: 11 Masses, 137 other liturgical works (sequences, antiphons, hymns, Magnificat settings, Litany of Loreto settings, Tenebrae lessons and responsories, Te Deum Settings); 84 Psalm settings; 207 motets (elevations, "Domine salvum" settings, occasional motets, dramatic motets ["oratorios"], miscellaneous motets).

Secular vocal works: 31 *airs sérieux et à boire*, 8 cantatas (Italian, French, and Latin).

Theatrical works: 15 pastorales, divertissements, and operas; overtures, *intermèdes*, and incidental music for 14 stage plays.

Instrumental works: 32 sacred compositions; 9 secular compositions.

Writings: Remarques sur les messes à 16 parties d'Italie: Règles de composition; Abrégé des règles de l'accompagnement.

Notes on *Pestis Mediolanensis*

General Background

Pestis Mediolanensis is one of a group of Charpentier's works commonly called oratorios (or, by the French, "histoires sacrées"). Charpentier himself did not use the term "oratorio"; he called these works variously *historia*, *canticum*, or *dialogus*. But he referred to compositions of all these types as motets, and we prefer to categorize them in general as "dramatic motets," indicating thereby both their character and their function. They were written for use in church or chapel services, although they were extraliturgical, and they functioned as did other occasional motets; virtually all of them can be related to specific feasts in the Church year. But they also belong to the Roman tradition of Latin dialogues and oratorios (to which Charpentier had been exposed as a student of Carissimi) in which solo singers personify individuals —and the chorus, groups of individuals—in a sacred story. The sources of such stories are the Bible (as in *Judicium Salomonis*, *Historia Esther*, or *Dialogus inter angelos et pastores Judeae in nativitatem Domini*), the lives of saints (as in *Caecilia virgo et martyr* or *In honorem sancti Ludovici regis Galliae*), or the imagination of one or another of the unidentified authors of their texts (as in *Dialogus inter esurientem, sitientem et Christum* or *Canticum pro pace*, in the latter of which the singers personify Peace, Justice, and an Angel).

Many of these motets are cast in dramatic form (often in two *partes*, like "acts"), with lively dialogue among the characters, but also with solo singers, ensembles, or choruses functioning as *historici* (narrators), since physical action had no place in their performance. Some among them, however, are less dramatic and more descriptive-narrative; this is true of *Pestis Mediolanensis*, as of such works as *Canticum in honorem Beatae Virginis Mariae* as well. Both types of works have prototypes among the Latin compositions of Carissimi, Charpentier's teacher and the source of his inspiration in the composition of dramatic motets.

Source and Dating

The unique source for *Pestis Mediolanensis* is a holograph score by Charpentier preserved among the "Mélanges autographes" (Paris, Bibl. Nat., Ms. Rés. Vm^1 259; 28 volumes). The main body of the work, without the prelude, is in Volume III, folios 120–30; preceding the score, a note by the composer reads, "Son prélude est dans le cahier XXIII," referring to a numbered manuscript fascicle now in Volume XVII, where on folios 41^v–42 we find the prelude, titled "Prélude pour Horrenda pestis." The score of the prelude offers alternative endings: in one, all parts have a full close, with a final measure of a full breve in each part (Charpentier's conventional ending for a work); in the other, which is marked "Au lieu de cette finale on peut jouer celle-ci, pour lier le motet avec le prélude," a half note in the three upper parts and a whole note in the bass replace the final breves of the first version, and the beginning of the opening vocal phrase ("Horrenda . . .") is cued. The present edition employs the second alternative, "to link the motet with the prelude."

The date of *Pestis Mediolanensis* is unknown. Understandably, it has been conjectured that it may have been composed for the centennial anniversary of the terrible plague of 1576–77 during which St. Charles Borromeo served in such a saintly and heroic way, or of the death of the saint himself (1584).[1] Internal evidence in Charpentier's manuscripts, however, suggests a date somewhere between these two, in the late 1670s. Such a date is arrived at through analysis of Charpentier's numbering of the fascicles ("cahiers") of his manuscripts. He numbered these manuscript fascicles consecutively, using, however, two sets of numerals, one arabic and the other roman; and, for reasons still unclear, the two series of fascicles thus numbered were composed more or less concurrently, not one after the other.

1. See below, p. 68; also H. Wiley Hitchcock, "The Latin Oratorios of Marc-Antoine Charpentier," *The Musical Quarterly*, XLI (1955), 41–65.

Some fascicles can be precisely dated, others only approximately. Cahier XXIII, which includes the prelude to *Pestis Mediolanensis*, dates from mid-1679, since it also includes music for a revival of Molière's play *Le sicilien* on 9 June of that year and since the next-numbered cahier (XXIV) includes music for a revival of the play *L'inconnu* on 17 October of the same year. Cahiers 23 and 24, on the other hand, containing the music of the motet proper, can be dated only approximately: they precede by a bit the precisely datable cahiers 28 and 29, including settings by Charpentier of responsories for Holy Week—which, however, according to a note in the manuscript he "did not complete . . . because of a change in the [Paris] Breviary" (a change which was made in 1680). Cahiers 23 and 24 thus cannot be dated more precisely than the late 1670s, and, since there is no proof that the prelude was composed at exactly the same time as the motet proper, one cannot be more specific than this for the entire work.

The Text

The scene described in the motet text is based on historical fact. In the summer of 1576, the dreaded bubonic plague that had already ravaged other north Italian cities struck Milan. It raged there for a half year; in early 1577 it began to abate, but only by early 1578 was it finally spent. Charles Borromeo (1538–1584) was Archbishop of Milan at the time. Away from the city when the pestilence broke out, he returned immediately, to lend sustenance and to comfort the victims. He made his will on 9 September 1576, then "gave himself up entirely to his people," making personal visits to plague-stricken homes and even to the hospital of St. Gregory, where the worst cases had been taken.[2] Partly because of his selflessness and charity during the plague, he was canonized on 1 November 1610, not long after his death, and 4 November was named the feast of St. Charles Borromeo.

The author of the motet text has not been identified. In form, it resembles those of other dramatic motets by Charpentier of the *canticum* type, although it lacks the personification of characters apparent in some of them. There are clearly three main divisions: one of narration, one of observation, and one of exhortation, which correspond to mm. 1–158, 159–263, and 264–340 of the music. The disposition of the text, with its mixture of Latin prose and rhymed verses of irregular lengths, is reminiscent of a number of the oratorio texts of Carissimi. The tone reflects a militant Counter-Reformation spirit and reminds one of the dramatic and varied appeals to the senses that were employed with cunning and cogency by the Jesuits, St. Philip Neri's Congregazione dell'Oratorio, and other agencies of the Counter-Reformation. This is especially apparent in the vivid portrayal of the plague-ridden city in the opening scene and the fervent, almost ecstatic language in which the praises of St. Charles are couched in the closing section.

The Music

Charpentier's musical setting responds faithfully to the structure and tone of the text, in each of its three sections.

An appropriately somber prelude opens the work and leads without pause into the setting of the opening "narrative" text passage (mm. 1–158). This is organized as a big *rondeau*-like unity in which the poetic refrain "Clamabant aegrotantium ora . . ." punctuates an ongoing, ever-building structure—Trio 1 (mm. 29–45) being followed by Trio 2 (mm. 78–89), Quartet 1 (mm. 114–35), Quartet 2 (mm. 141–47), and finally a double quartet (mm. 148–58) which itself concludes with a variant of the refrain. The key Charpentier chooses is C minor, which for him was one of an "obscure and sad" affect.[3] In the lamenting refrain, drooping suspensions on "clamabant" (echoed in two ritornels for flutes and continuo which help to organize the *rondeau*) and gasping pauses in the middle of the

---

2. *The Catholic Encyclopaedia, s.v.* "Charles Borromeo."

3. Marc-Antoine Charpentier, *Règles de composition* (Paris, Bibl. Nat., MS, *nouv. acq. fr.* 6355), fols. 13–13ᵛ; see also Hitchcock, "The Latin Oratorios." Despite his theoretical distinctions among keys and modes, Charpentier was not above transposition if practical considerations invited it; see Hitchcock, "Some Aspects of Notation in an *Alma Redemptoris Mater* (c. 1670) by Marc-Antoine Charpentier (d. 1704)," *Notations and Editions*, ed. Edith Borroff (Dubuque: Wm. C. Brown, 1974), pp. 127–34.

word "suspirabant" (sighed) intensify the dolorous atmosphere.

The text passage of "observation," in which St. Charles is seen coming to the aid of the dying plague victims, is set in two subsections by Charpentier, again in response to the text. The first of these (mm. 159–89), setting the prose sentence beginning "Afflictionem miseri populi," is for double chorus and full orchestra. The second subsection (mm. 190–263) is another *rondeau*-like structure (responding to the series of three parallel five-line poetic stanzas beginning at "Infirmos languentes") for vocal duets accompanied only by continuo, with instrumental ritornels between the stanzas that relate back musically to the ritornels in the first section of the piece. For the culminating three-line stanza ("O magna pietas! . . .") Charpentier adds a third singer.

The final section of "exhortation," calling for the faithful to sing St. Charles's praises, is yet another *rondeau*, with double chorus and orchestra alternating with *couplets* (contrast episodes) for soloists. The mood shifts to one of jubilation, through changes of meter, tempo, and mode (to C major, which was for Charpentier a "gay and warlike" key).

Charpentier's debt to Italian music—specifically to Carissimi's but also to mid-*seicento* music in general—is apparent in any number of stylistic details. The opening prelude, in a simple and clear binary form (A A') with coda, is akin to several preludes to Latin works by Carissimi and may even be compared, in length, texture, and design, to such an opera overture as that by Monteverdi for *L'Incoronazione di Poppea*. The vocal solos and solo ensembles are in two basic styles also rooted in the Italian cantata/opera manner of mid-century Rome and Venice. One, exemplified by the two opening tenor solos, is essentially recitative, but a *recitativo arioso* made musically more interesting and shapely by use of melodic sequences. The other, exemplified by the refrain of the first section ("Clamabant aegrotantium ora"), is an even more "airy" triple-meter, cantabile style. The choral recitative of the second section ("Afflictionem miseri populi") may also be traced to Carissimi, especially its strong, simple rhythms and the high incidence of hammering dactyls ("Fervidus volat, anxius currit") in it. And the polychoral antiphony of the same chorus (and of the final one as well) also has its prototypes in Carissimi's and other Romans' Latin works.

Details of word-painting, too, link Charpentier with an Italian tradition descended from the sixteenth-century madrigal: besides the gasping, broken utterance of "suspirabant" cited above, we might point to the contrast between the paired imitation with which Charpentier portrays "fathers and mothers" (mm. 114–28) and the imitation between single voices, immediately following, with which he limns "husband and wife," or to the melismata with which he underscores jubilant words like "fervens" (mm. 250ff. and later mm. 327ff.) and "gloriae" (mm. 306ff.).

The Present Edition

Performing Forces

It will be convenient, in discussing the performing forces of *Pestis Mediolanensis*, to refer to some critical points in the score, in the original notation (Examples 1–7). These excerpts have been chosen also with a view to showing details of the original manuscript—clefs, time-signatures, cues for instrumental doubling, *croches blanches* (see below, under "Time-Signatures and Tempos"), and the like—which are often included in *incipits* at section-beginnings in scholarly editions. It is intended thereby to discharge scholarly responsibilities while leaving the music pages uncluttered with such *incipits*.

The prelude is scored in four parts (Example 1).

Example 1

No instruments are designated, but the clefs—French violin (first-line G), soprano, mezzo-soprano, and bass—are those commonly employed by Charpentier for an instrumental ensemble of violin-family strings (as opposed to viols, for which he uses different clefs). These string parts would have been termed by Charpentier *dessus*, *haute-contre*, *taille*, and *basse*[1] or *premier dessus*, *second dessus*, *haute-contre*, and *basse*.[2] In the Lullian five-part orchestra, the three inner parts (termed *haute-contre*, *taille*, and *quinte*) were played by instruments tuned a fifth below the violin, that is, like a viola.[3] In Charpentier's typical (and more Italianate) four-part orchestral scoring, however, the second part (with soprano clef) lies in the mid-violin range (in *Pestis Mediolanensis*, from f^1 up to $e^{\flat 2}$, and even the third part (mezzo-soprano clef) seldom drops below the low open g of the violin (in *Pestis Mediolanensis*, the range is from g to a^1). Thus in this edition I have transcribed the four parts as for string quartet. (It should be noted, however, that the bass part was probably conceived for the French *basse de violon*—a larger instrument, and one tuned a whole tone lower, than a cello.)

"Flûtes" are called for, as I have noted, in the series of ritornels beginning at m. 72 (see Example 2).

Example 2

Charpentier undoubtedly had recorders in mind, since when he wishes transverse flutes he specifies them (as *flûtes d'Allemagne* or *flûtes allemandes*; other French composers refer also to *flûtes traversières*). With flutes specifically demanded in this passage, we can assume that when "tous les instruments" are to double the voices (as at m. 159; see Example 3) the

---

1. As, for example, in the separate parts, almost all in Charpentier's hand, of *Judicium Salomonis* (Paris, Bibl. Nat., Vm¹ 1481).

2. As, for example, in the separate parts, almost all in Charpentier's hand, of the Mass *Assumpta est Maria* (Paris, Bibl. Nat., Vm¹ 942).

3. The evidence for this is summarized in James R. Anthony, *French Baroque Music*, 2nd ed. (New York: W. W. Norton, 1978), p. 95.

Example 3

two upper string parts are to be doubled by flutes, and in these passages the present edition calls for such doubling. It would not be inappropriate even to add doubling oboes in these *tous* (the French equivalent of *tutti*) passages.

The bass instrumental part, although unfigured in the prelude, has some figuration in the motet proper. Thus it is a *basse continue*, and in fact an organ is cited in the score at m. 156 (see Example 4). A cello or *basse de violon* should join the organ bass in solo vocal and small-ensemble passages; all the orchestral bass strings should play in the *tous* passages; and, given the presence of doubling winds in the upper parts, a doubling bassoon or two may also be employed (just as one bassoon, substituting for a cello, may also be employed in the ritornels for flutes alone).

The vocal parts eventually add up to a double chorus *a 8* (SATB/SATB), at m. 159 (see Example 3); this is to be doubled by instruments, as the note at m. 159—"Toutes les voix et tous les instruments"—indicates. The instrumental parts are not, however, written out and must be added editorially, as I have done in the "grand choeur" of mm. 159–89 and in the last section of the motet (mm. 264ff.), which Charpentier heads with the note, "Voix et instruments." In these choral passages, as well as some for vocal ensembles, Charpentier economizes by making the lowermost staff serve for both continuo and vocal bass parts (see Examples 3 and 5). In this edition, I have consistently written out a separate continuo part, simplifying the rhythms where appropriate, so that the continuo part does not constantly parrot the text-rhythms.

From the double chorus, Charpentier extracts a double quartet (also SATB/SATB). Soloists from the *premier choeur* (first chorus) he indicates with the letter "a" (Examples 5, 6, and 7), those from the *second choeur* with the letter "b" (Example 5). In the present edition, I replace these letter-indications

Example 4

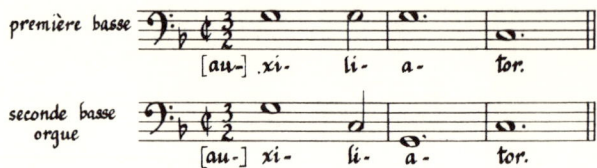

Example 5

Example 6

Example 7

with the currently more conventional numbers: soprano soloists 1 and 2, tenor soloists 1 and 2, and so on.

If, as we imagine, *Pestis Mediolanensis* was composed for church use, Charpentier probably wrote it with male voices only in mind (boys and men). In present-day performance of the choral passages, the use of female voices for the two upper parts (*dessus* and *haute-contre*—treble and high tenor) of each choir poses no problems, and in the edition these parts have both been transcribed in treble clef. In the solo and ensemble passages, however, the use of a high tenor (rather than a female contralto) for any *haute-contre* part is distinctly desirable, especially in such characteristic trio passages as in mm. 55–71 and 91–107 or the double duet of mm. 114–35. The trios invite the homogeneous sonority of an all-male ensemble; the double duet, on the other hand, invites a contrast between the two sopranos and the two lower voices. Accordingly, in this edition solo "alto" parts—that is, those for *haute-contre*—have been assigned to a high tenor and transcribed in [treble-8] clef. (All actual tenor parts have been similarly transcribed.)

The two flutes called for specifically in the score for use in the ritornels of mm. 72–77 (Example 2) and its variant in mm. 109–13 might also be used for the similar ritornels of mm. 204–7 (see Example 7), 221–24, 238–41, and 258–63. However, the instrumentation of the latter ritornels is not designated by Charpentier, and for variety I have suggested for them a pair of violins (equally appropriate).

In sum, *Pestis Mediolanensis*, as it is edited here, calls for a double quartet of vocal soloists, double chorus *a 8*, two recorders, two solo violins, double string orchestra *a 8* (with recorders and perhaps oboes doubling the two upper parts of each sub-orchestra), and a continuo group of an organ, a bass string instrument, and perhaps a bassoon or two in the *tous* passages.

Time-Signatures and Tempos

The time-signatures appearing in the work are 2, C, 3, and ₵³⁄₂. With the signature ₵³⁄₂, Charpentier employs "white eighths" (*croches blanches*: ♪) and "white sixteenths" (♪) (see Examples 5 and 7). This notational convention is, of course, no longer in use, and in this edition the signature ³⁄₂ has been substituted for ₵³⁄₂ and the rhythmic notation modernized. The hemiola cadences common to such triple meters, in which ³⁄₂ shifts effectively, for a moment, to ³⁄₁ in Charpentier's music (as in others'), are indicated in square brackets above the staff (see mm. 123–27 of the edition).

Although one should not be too rigidly prescriptive about it, a certain degree of proportional relationship between passages with the four different time-signatures (2, C, 3, and ₵³⁄₂) exists in Charpentier's music, as in other French music of his time. Such a relationship has a bearing, of course, on the tempos. As I have suggested elsewhere, 2 (= ²⁄₂) signifies a measure of two slow beats; its relationship to C is 2♩ = C♩ and, to ₵³⁄₂, 2♩ = ₵³⁄₂♩.[4] Assuming a "slow" beat to be about M.M. 60–72, there is no need to reduce note-values in editing the work. It is hard to imagine that in the later passages of the motet, with their atmosphere of jubilation and excitement, the basic tempos should not be speeded up, especially with the appearance of the fast triple-meter signature 3 (= ³⁄₄). Such an increase has been indicated editorially (as have other metronomic tempo suggestions).

Other Editorial Commentary

Besides the editorial additions and alterations already commented upon, suggestions of dynamics, additional ornamentation, and additional bass figuration have been made in the edition in square brackets. Three signs for ornaments appear in the manuscript; these are as follows (with suggested realizations in parentheses):

---

4. Hitchcock, "Some Aspects of Notation."

The trills begin on the beat, not before it.

Editorial slurs are given in dotted lines (⌢⌢⌢).

Following the end of the manuscript (and preceding a giant, scrawled "fin de la Peste de Milan") is the composer's note, " 'Hymnum ergo' et toute la suite se recommence et les trois a [soloists 1] disent les récits des trois b [soloists 2]; et l'on finit par le grand 'Hymnum' par où l'on a commencé" ('Hymnum ergo' and all that follows is repeated, with soloists 1 taking the place of soloists 2; and the work is concluded with the great 'Hymnum' with which [the last section] began). Accordingly, the conclusion of the motet is to go as follows:

(1) mm. 264–340, the three soloists being Tenor 2, Bass 2, and High Tenor 2, respectively;

(2) mm. 264–340 repeated, the three soloists being Tenor 1, Bass 1, and High Tenor 1, respectively;

(3) mm. 264–89 repeated.

The following errors in the manuscript have been corrected:

m. 1, Violin 2: B♭

m. 28, Violin 2: A♮

m. 43, High Tenor: last note is E♮

m. 95, High Tenor: ♪♪ on last beat; changed by analogy with mm. 60, 140

m. 155, Soprano 1: last note is E♮

m. 169, Choir 2, alto and tenor at "gentis":

(not an error, but awkward if female voices are used for alto part)

m. 176, Choir 2, alto: first three notes are E♮

m. 182, Choir 1, alto: first half of measure is ♩ 𝄾

m. 235, High Tenor: last note is E♮

m. 303, bass soloist: Bass I, only, is indicated; changed in the light of the composer's note regarding the conclusion of the work (quoted above)

Previous Edition; Phonorecording

About 1900, Charles Bordes published *Pestis Mediolanensis* under the title *La Peste de Milan* as Number 2 in a group of three dramatic motets (*histoires sacrées*) by Charpentier (the others being, as titled by Bordes, *Dialogue entre Madeleine et Jésus* and *Le Reniement de St Pierre*), in a series sponsored by the Schola Cantorum in Paris, "Concerts Spirituels (Série Ancienne)—Documents pour servir à l'histoire de la musique religieuse de Concert, publiés d'après les éditions originales et les manuscrits." Bordes's edition, although not without some merits, is faulty in several respects: it omits mm. 159–340 (or more than half the composition); it transposes the music, without acknowledgment, down a semitone (possibly because Bordes knew that the pitch in seventeenth-century Parisian churches was lower than $a^1 = 440$); and in mm. 136–58 it misrepresents the double solo quartet as a *petit choeur* of four soloists plus a choral *grand choeur a 8*.

A phonorecording based on the present edition was made in 1971 by the Musica Aeterna Chamber Orchestra and Chorus, Frederic Waldman conducting (Decca DL 79437).

Text of *Pestis Mediolanensis*

Horrenda pestis Mediolanum vastabat;
   non aetati, non generi, non sexui parcebat.
Ubique luctus, ubique timor,
   ubique planctus, ubique tremor.

Dispersa erant in capite omnium platearum cadavera,
   et foedis odoribus mortis contagia late spargebant.
   Sed heu, heu! quod flebilius, quod miserius,
   quod funestius!

Clamabant aegrotantium ora,
   suspirabant morientium pectora,
     et non erat auxiliator.

Salutem suam curabat unusquisque. Extinctus erat
   amor proximi, extincta penitus charitas. Servi
   a dominis, pauperes a divitibus miserationem
   expostulabant. A famulis domini, ab amicis amici
   solamen petebant.

Clamabant aegrotantium ora,
   suspirabant morientium pectora,
     et non erat auxiliator.

Patres et matres a natis, nati pariter a parentibus
   auxilium quaerebant. Sponsus ab uxora, uxor a
   sponso poscebat opem.

Clamabant aegrotantium ora,
   suspirabant morientium pectora,
     et non erat auxiliator.

Afflictionem miseri populi ut audivit magnus Dei
   servus Carolus, ad auxilium desperatae gentis
   properat, anxius currit, fervidus volat.

Infirmos languentes
   solatur hortatur
     et plagas madentes
        tergit osculatur.
           O magna pietas!

A terrible plague was ravaging Milan;
   neither age, nor rank, nor sex did it respect.
Everywhere mourning, everywhere fear,
   everywhere wailing, everywhere trembling.

Corpses were strewn at the head of every street,
   and contagion spread far and wide by the fetid
   odors of death. But alas, alas! even more grievous,
   more miserable, more melancholy!

Cries rose from the mouths of the sick,
   sighs from the breasts of the dying,
     and there was no one to help.

Each one thought only of helping himself. Love of
   neighbor was forgotten, charity [too] forgotten
   totally. Servants from masters, the poor from the
   rich, sought compassion. Masters of their servants,
   friends of friends, begged for relief.

Cries rose from the mouths of the sick,
   sighs from the breasts of the dying,
     and there was no one to help.

Fathers and mothers of their children, children
   equally of their parents, pleaded for help. Husband
   of wife, wife of husband, begged for assistance.

Cries rose from the mouths of the sick,
   sighs from the breasts of the dying,
     and there was no one to help.

When Charles, the great servant of God, heard the
   torment of the wretched people, he hurried to the
   aid of the desperate ones; solicitous, he hastened;
   eager, he flew.

The languishing sick
   he soothed, encouraged,
     and the streaming wounds
        he cleansed with kisses.
           O great piety!

In terram prostratus
  cum vultu sereno
    quamvis purpuratus
      inservit egeno.
        O summa humilitas!

Quod parens recondit
  argentum et aurum
   his laetus effundit
    pater miserorum.
      O fervens charitas!

O magna pietas!
  O summa humilitas!
    O fervens charitas!

Hymnum ergo cantemus in honorem beati Caroli.
Celebramus eum, jubilemus, exultemus in solemnitate illius.

Illum magna pietas sanctorum inseruit choro.
Hymnum ergo cantemus in honorem beati Caroli.

Illum summa humilitas gloriae subvexit thoro.
Celebramus eum, jubilemus, exultemus in solemnitate illius.

Illum fervens charitas velut solum inter beatorum agmina affixit coelo.

Hymnum ergo cantemus in honorem beati Caroli.
Celebramus eum, jubilemus, exultemus in solemnitate illius.

Prostrate on the ground,
  with serene countenance,
    though clad in purple
      he served the poor.
        O highest humility!

Whereas parents withheld
  silver and gold,
    this father of the wretched
      poured it forth joyously.
        O fervent charity!

O great piety!
  O highest humility!
    O fervent charity!

Therefore let us sing a hymn in honor of the blessed Charles.
Let us sing his praises, let us rejoice and exult on his feast day.

Great piety put him in the choir of the saints.
Therefore let us sing a hymn in honor of the blessed Charles.

Highest humility carried him up to the throne of glory.
Let us sing his praises, let us rejoice and exult on his feast day.

Fervent charity placed him, alone as it were, in heaven among the throngs of the blessed.

Therefore let us sing a hymn in honor of the blessed Charles.
Let us sing his praises, let us rejoice and exult on his feast day.[1]

---

1. For assistance with both the Latin text and its translation, I am grateful to Professor Virginia Brown of the Pontifical Institute of Mediaeval Studies, Toronto, Canada.

Score of *Pestis Mediolanensis*

Suivez au grand chœur:

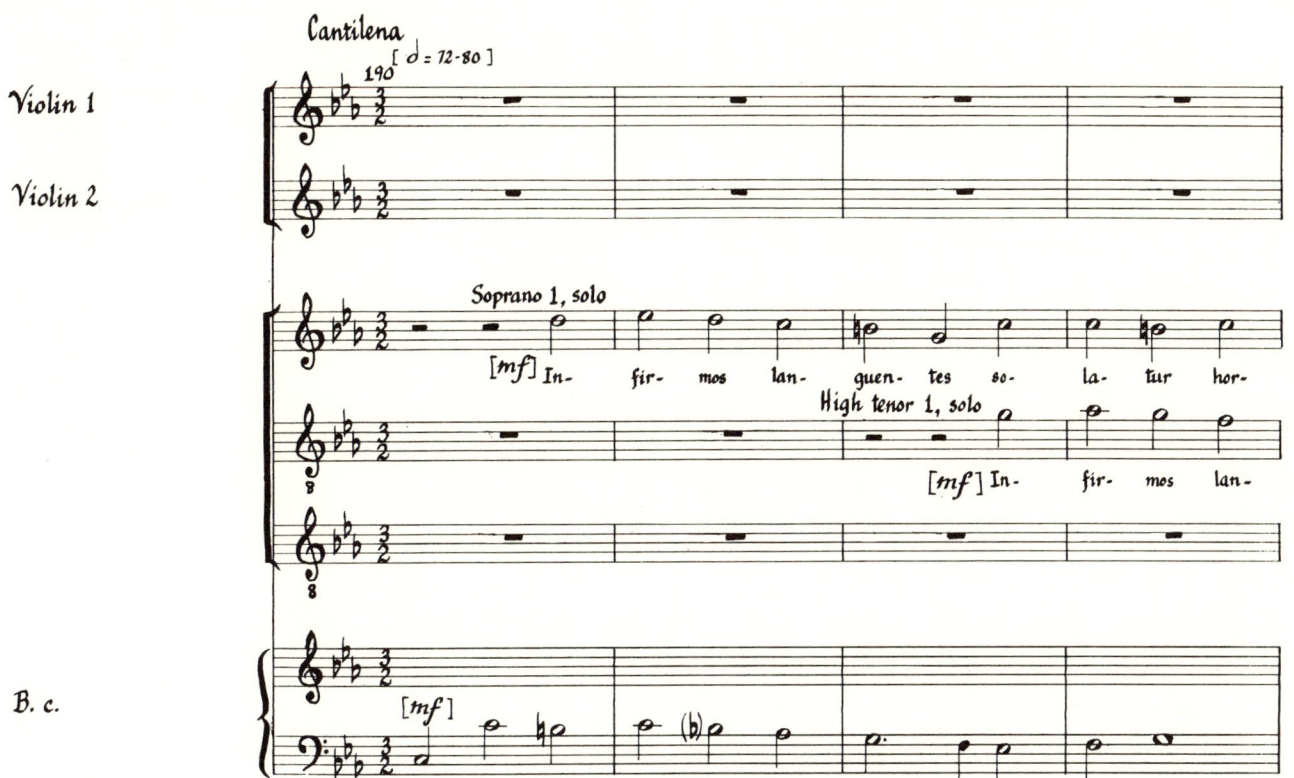

44

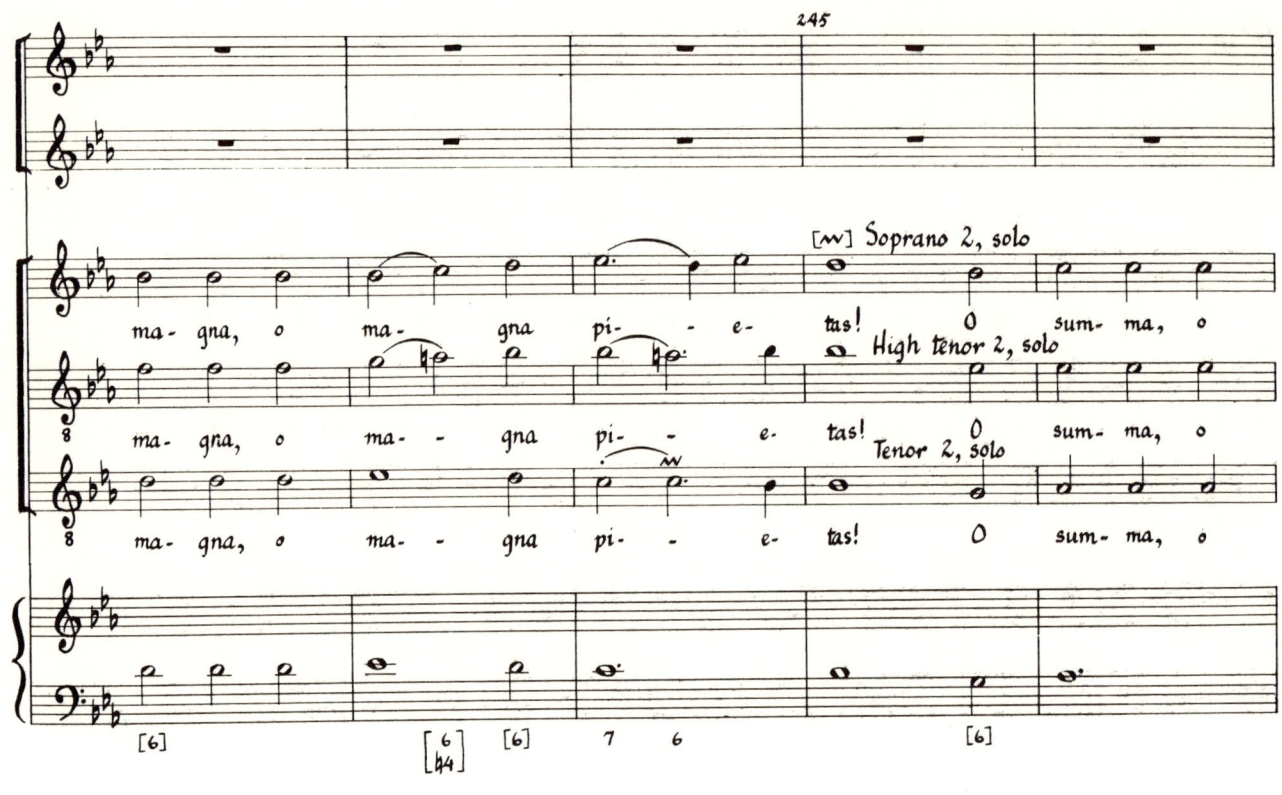

48

[♩= 120-126]

1st time: Tenor 2, solo
2nd time: Tenor 1, solo
[mf]

Il- lum ma- gna pi- e- tas sanc- to- rum in- se- ru- it

[mf]

Readings

André Maugars
[*from* Reply to a Person Curious About the Nature of Italian Music, *written at Rome, 1 October 1639*][1]

The long open letter by Maugars, French gamba player, reporting back to his compatriots on the new Italian music he had experienced during a stay in Rome of more than a year, is full of interesting observations. His remarks on Italian sacred music, on the "recitative style" (totally new to him, as it would have been to other French visitors to Italy in 1638–39), and on performances of oratorios at San Marcello are relevant here since they deal with a musical scene that Charpentier would have been part of—somewhat later, to be sure—as a student of Carissimi in Rome. In fact, some of the oratorios heard and cited by Maugars may have been by Carissimi, who was commissioned for a number of works by the Archconfraternity of the Holy Cross.

. . . I have finally resolved to write frankly to you my opinions on Italian music and the differences I find between it and our own [French music], enjoining you . . . to judge in good faith this little musical essay. I intend, therefore, to tell you today, impartially and openly, without holding anything back, what I have learned from the experience of twelve or fifteen months spent in Italy among the most excellent persons in the art, during which I have attended diligently the most celebrated concerts given in Rome.

To begin with, I find that their sacred music has much more art, science, and variety than ours, but also more freedom. . . . Our composers . . . remain too scrupulously constrained by pedantic considerations and . . . think they violate the rules of the art if they allow two fifths in succession, or if they depart, no matter how slightly, from their modes. [But] a judicious man, skilled in his craft, is not sentenced without parole to remain always in a narrow cell; he can skilfully escape, if his imagination leads him to some nice discovery, or if the quality of the text or the beauty of the parts demands it. This is what the Italians practice so well. . . . Thus it is that they compose their motets with more art, more science, more variety, and more agreeableness than ours.

Besides these great advantages that they have over us, what makes their music still more agreeable is that they exercise much more care in their performances and place the choirs better than we do, assigning to each one a small organ, which without doubt helps them to sing with better intonation.

. . . There is [one] kind of music [here] which is not at all in use in France and for that reason merits a special account from me. It is called recitative style. The best that I heard was in the oratory of San Marcello, where there is a congregation of Brothers of the Holy Cross made up of the greatest Roman noblemen, who therefore have the power to command all the rarest [talents] that Italy produces; and indeed the most excellent musicians are at pains to be seen there, and the proudest composers court the honor of having their works performed there, and try to display there the very best of their learning.

This admirable and ravishing music is to be heard only on Lenten Fridays, from three until six o'clock. The church is not nearly as large as the Sainte-Chapelle in Paris. At one end of it there is a spacious platform with an organ of average size, very delicate in tone and well suited to voices. At the sides of the church there are furthermore two other small stages, where the finest of instrumentalists were [placed]. The singers began with a psalm in the

---

1. *Response faite à un curieux sur le sentiment de la musique d'Italie escrite à Rome le 1ᵉʳ octobre 1639* (n.p., n.d.). Excerpts translated for this volume by the editor from the copy in the Bibliothèque Mazarine, Paris. The *Response* was republished in Ernest Thoinan, *Maugars, célèbre joueur de viole* (Paris: A. Claudin, 1865).

form of a motet, and then all the instruments played a fine piece [*symphonie*]. Then the voices sang a tale from the Old Testament in the form of a religious drama, like that of Susanna [and the Elders], of Judith and Holofernes, [or] of David and Goliath. Each singer represented a character in the story and expressed perfectly the spirit of the text. Then one of the most celebrated preachers delivered the sermon, after which the music recounted [*récitoit*] the gospel for the day, such as the story of the Samaritan woman, of the woman of Canaan, of Lazarus, of the Magdalene, or of the Passion of Our Lord, the singers imitating very skilfully the various characters delineated by the evangelist. I cannot praise this recitative music enough; one must hear it in person to appreciate its merits. . . .

Sébastien de Brossard
[*from* Dictionary of Music, 1703][2]

Brossard's invaluable dictionary is of special interest to students of late seventeenth-century music in France, with its musico-political struggles between adherents of a pure French music unsullied by Italianisms and others who appreciated and welcomed the brilliant and sensuous charms of Italian seicento *music. The dictionary was, among other things, an attempt by a lively, broad-minded, and literate musician to familiarize his French readers with the concepts and terminology of Italian music (Brossard himself being very partial to it) as well as to define systematically contemporaneous French music theory and nomenclature. Brossard's entries for "motet" and "oratorio," which overlap at several points, suggest how a work like* Pestis Mediolanensis *might have been called by either name.*

MOTETTO, plural Motetti. Others write Motteto, others Moteto, etc.; in Latin, Motettus, or Mottetus, Motectum, Muteta, Canticum, Modulus, etc.; in French, MOTET. It is a very elaborate musical composition, enriched with the greatest refinements of the art of composition, for 1, 2, 3, 4, 5, 6, 7, 8, and even more voices or parts, often with instruments but ordinarily, in fact almost always, with at least a basso continuo, etc. And all this on a very brief subject [*une Période fort courte*], whence according to some comes the name Motet, as if it were but one *Mot*. When the composer takes the liberty of employing in it all that comes to mind without applying any words to it or subjecting himself to expressing their sense or feeling, the Italians then call it Fantasia or Ricercata; the French, Fantaisie, Recherche, etc.

At present, the meaning of this term is extended to all pieces based on Latin texts, no matter on what subject, such as praise of saints, elevations, etc. Entire psalms are even set in the form of motets, etc.

ORATORIO. It is a sort of spiritual opera made up of dialogues, solos, duets, trios, ritornels, full choruses, etc., the subject of which is taken either from the Scriptures or from the life of some saint. Or else it is an allegory on one of the religious mysteries, or some matter of morals, etc. Its music must be enriched with all the refinements and subtleties of the art. The text is almost always drawn from Holy Writ. There are many with texts in Italian, and they may be in French. Nothing is more common in Rome, especially during Lent, than these sorts of Oratorio. One of great beauty by M[onsieur Jacques François] Lochon was just presented to the public [*Oratorio pour la naissance de l'Enfant Jésus*, published in Lochon's *Motets en musique* . . . of 1701]; it is for four voices and two violins.

2. *Dictionaire de musique* . . . (Paris: Christophe Ballard, 1703, reprinted Amsterdam: Antiqua, 1964). Excerpts translated for this volume by the editor.

Sébastien de Brossard
[*from Brossard's catalogue of his music collection*]³

Brossard was an avid collector of musical scores, part-books, and theoretical works. The manuscript catalogue of his collection is full of interesting comments not only on the music and books in it but their composers and authors as well. In his entry for the copy of the 1694 publication of the score of Charpentier's Médée *that he owned, we find many illuminating remarks about its composer by one who viewed his music sympathetically.*

This M. Charpentier, whom I believe to be Parisian, lived for several years in Rome, where he was a most assiduous disciple and emulator of the famous Carissimi. I am assured of one thing that may be difficult to believe: he had a prodigious memory, and once having heard a piece of music he could write it out completely. Thus it is that the motets *Vidi impium*, *Emendemus in melius*, and others and several oratorios of Carissimi, which were never printed, got to France —at least, that is what is claimed.

On his return from Italy he worked for some time for the Comédie-Française [*les Comédiens françois*; i.e., Molière's troupe]. . . . In addition, he produced a number of other works, both sacred and secular, of uncommon excellence, which are catalogued below under "Manuscripts" (for few things of his have been published).

Because of his Italian experience during his youth, some French [critics]—parochial or, to speak more plainly, jealous of the excellence of his music— have had occasion to reproach him for his Italianate taste (most inopportunely, for he has chosen only the best from them; his works attest to this).

Whatever may be the case, he has always been considered, in the judgment of true connoisseurs, as the most profound and learned of modern musicians. This, without doubt, is why the Jesuits of rue Saint-Antoine chose him as music-master of their church—a post at that time among the most brilliant ones—and, even more notable, why the Duke of Chartres (later Duke of Orléans and Regent of France) selected him to be his teacher of the fundamentals of music composition. . . .

To return to his opera *Circé* [*recte Médée*], it is without a doubt the most learned and subtle of all those that have been published, at least since the death of Lully, although because of cabals of the envious and ignorant it was not as well received by the public as it deserved to be (along with many others). From this one, more than from any other opera, without exception, the things most essential to good composition may be learned. Thus for a long time I was unsure whether I should not catalogue it under the theoreticians—that is to say, among the masters of the art of music—rather than in the category of ordinary operas.

Michel Brenet
[*from "Marc-Antoine Charpentier"*]⁴

Michel Brenet (a pseudonym for Marie Bobillier) was the first modern musicologist to insist on the importance of Charpentier and to encourage a revival of his music. It was at her instigation that the first modern performances and editions of works of Charpentier were undertaken by Charles Bordes at the Schola Cantorum in Paris in the late 1890s and early 1900s. Not by chance did Bordes perform and publish three of Charpentier's dramatic motets, including Pestis Mediolanensis: *Brenet emphasized in her critical writings about Charpentier that he was "above all, a dramatist," and it would have been natural for her to suggest that Bordes concern himself with the* histoires sacrées *or* dialogues *among the sacred works. The following excerpts are from Brenet's first account of Charpentier's life and music.*

---

3. *Catalogue des livres de musique théorique et pratique, vocale et instrumentale . . . qui sont dans le cabinet du Sr Sébastien de Brossard . . .* (1724) (Paris, Bibl. Nat., Ms. Rés. Vm⁸ 21). Excerpts translated for this volume by the editor.

4. *La Tribune de Saint-Gervais*, VI/3 (March 1900), 65–76. Excerpts translated for this volume by the editor.

. . . The dramatic sense that informs even the least of Charpentier's works, including his sacred compositions, demonstrates how he would have been able to develop a strong personal style in the theater and to gain renown there if Lully's jealousy had not completely shut him, as well as other French masters, out of the Opéra. . . .

. . . We might very probably name one or the other of the great psalms for soloists, chorus, and orchestra that are scattered among the twenty-eight volumes of the "Mélanges [autographes]", which correspond exactly to the forms used in the royal chapel, as having been written for the chapel of the Dauphin. But it is not at all among them that one should seek Charpentier's originality—that originality which some have claimed to have been willed, out of hate for or opposition to Lully, but which in our opinion was natural and spontaneous. Rather, one finds it and admires it in the nonliturgical sacred works that are found among his manuscripts side by side with the Masses, the hymns, and the motets, and that for the most part he had occasion to write while in the service of the Jesuits. These were now Latin cantatas on subjects *d'occasion* (a lament on the death of Queen Marie-Thérèse, 1683; expressions of thanks for the recovery of the Dauphin and others for that of the King, dating from 1696 [*recte* early 1680s and 1686, respectively]; a psalm *in tempore belli, pro Rege*; series of choral and instrumental movements for the consecration of a bishop or for a procession); now dialogues or cantatas for the feasts of Christmas, the Circumcision, Easter, St. Louis, or St. Francis Xavier; now—finally and especially— oratorios, in which Charpentier carried on the semireligious and semitheatrical tendencies of his master, Carissimi.

Like most French composers, Charpentier was, above all, a dramatist and a colorist. In sacred music, to which he found himself dedicated as much by the external circumstances of his life as by inner calling, what attracted him most, what responded best to his artistic nature, was not liturgical texts of a general, abstract character, in which the idea is both impersonal and universal; it was rather subjects with a more objective essence, where the text suggests and permits the expression of particular, precise feelings. This is why the form of oratorio, or more exactly of the *histoire sacrée* such as Carissimi had cultivated, accorded perfectly with the aspirations and temperament of Charpentier. His compositions in this genre, all unpublished (and, we might add, unknown) constitute in our opinion the finest part of his oeuvre. Their subjects are episodes chosen from the Old and New Testaments; their texts are chapters from Holy Scripture (or at least closely related verses without extraneous lyric additions) distributed among the "historian" or narrator, the chorus, and the various interlocutors in the action. Such are *The Judgment of Solomon*, *The Sacrifice of Abraham*, *Joshua*, the story of *Judith* and that of *Esther*, *The Prodigal Son*, *The Death of Saul and Jonathan*, *The Fight between St. Michael and the Dragon*, *The Birth of Jesus Christ*, *The Circumcision*, *The Massacre of the Innocents*, *Dialogue between Jesus and the Magdalene*, *The Betrayal of St. Peter*, *The Resurrection*, and *The Last Judgment*. To these should be added *St. Cecilia, Virgin and Martyr* and *The Plague of Milan*—which, musically, spring from the same domain—and, if you like, *Epitaphium Carpentarij*, a curious little cantata, half-humorous, half-melancholy, in which the composer has his ghost sing, giving it as interlocutors Ignatius, Marcellus, and a choir of angels.

Only one of these works is dated: this is *The Judgment of Solomon*, of which the [sub]title—*Motet pour la messe rouge du Palais en 1702*—also tells us that, at that time, the early oratorio—the *histoire sacrée*— based exclusively (from a textual standpoint) on passages of Holy Writ and considered as a motet, had not yet exited from the church. It held there a position analogous to that of the *grand motet* for soloists, chorus, and orchestra (whose dimensions it by no means exceeded), a position distinctly extra-liturgical (hence debatable) which had been accorded it without resistance, since the ritualistic flavor of Catholic music was changing under the increasing influence of dramatic music. A new conception of religious art had sprung up among the masters of the seventeenth century. They saw it now in expressive terms. Instead of the seraphic fervor of Palestrinian polyphony, prayer for them expressed human anguish and passion; in breaking new paths, they discovered unknown beauties, less pure but more moving. Perhaps more than any other French master of the time, Charpentier personified this new ideal. And no one acquainted with *Le Reniement de St Pierre*, having read or heard especially the chorus to the words of St. Matthew and St. Luke, "Et recordatus est Petrus verbi Jesu, et egressus foras flevit amare," which ends this brief, admirable, and poignant work, will deny to the musician who signed it the gift of genius.

Clarence H. Barber
[from "The Oratorios of Marc-Antoine Charpentier"][5]

Clarence Barber was one of several American musicologists who, in the 1950s and 1960s, contributed to a second revival of interest in, and publication and recording of, Charpentier's music. Some of the facts in the lengthy article from which the following is extracted have been shown, through later research, to be in error, but Professor Barber's insightful remarks on Pestis Mediolanensis *remain a valuable contribution.*

. . . Neither Lully's monopoly over the theater nor the specialization outside of it that was forced on Charpentier sufficed to destroy the fundamentally *dramatic* qualities of his art: throughout his sacred works, there is found an astonishing series of pieces of a "scenic" character, a series that begins even when our young musician, seventeen years of age, is pursuing his studies in Italy . . . and one that will extend to the end of his life (1704) at the Sainte-Chapelle, following the period with the Princess de Guise (1680–1688) and that with the Jesuits (1684–1698). These works are as rich in contrasts, development, and colorful tableaux as the noble operas of Jean-Baptiste Lully—or as the *Médée* of Charpentier himself.

We shall discover in these "oratorios" of Charpentier a truly masterful gift for storytelling, for evoking emotion, and for tone-painting. And we shall see—or rather the present article will seek to have us see—the diversity, the beauty, and the variety of his religious music (at least of the different kinds of works that are subsumed under the name "oratorio").

. . . In reviewing the oratorios of Marc-Antoine Charpentier, we shall see that this term excludes neither the motet nor the Passion nor the cantata. We shall also see that despite a certain analogy with opera, the oratorio in France during the reign of the Sun King includes neither costumes nor stage sets. And if occasionally it finds a place in liturgical ceremony (as is true of the elevations), it can also be performed outside the church (*Mors Saulis et Jonathae*).

[Professor Barber continues with a lengthy discussion of Charpentier's oratorio production, based on the present editor's classification of the oratorios according to three types—*historiae, cantica*, and *dialogi*. The remarks on the second of these types begin with a consideration of *Pestis Mediolanensis*.]

To place *The Plague of Milan* (*Pestis Mediolanensis*) chronologically, we would hazard the date 1684, centenary of the death of St. Charles Borromeo, the Milanese saint whose life was so intimately linked with that baleful event—a guess reinforced by the fact that the previous year, 1683, saw the beginning of the association between our composer and the Jesuits. On the other hand, certain stylistic details would suggest that *The Plague* had been composed at a considerably earlier time. Other occasions than the centenary of St. Charles might, after all, have given rise to the work: the anniversary of the plague itself [1576–77], a celebration of the annual feast-day of the saint, a commission from an individual saved from death in battle or from a serious illness; or it may simply have been a *pièce d'occasion* commissioned by some wealthy patron belonging to one of the various Italian families resident in Paris. And might we not, in fact, imagine that Charpentier remained below the Alps longer than he is said to have, attached to some provincial court or obscure church, and that such a work had been requested of him? . . .

. . . One slightly disturbing thing is that there is a certain stylistic affinity between *The Betrayal* [*of St. Peter*] and *The Plague*. Both reveal the influence of Carissimi: *The Plague* calls for a very limited number of obbligato instruments: [it has] a prelude of indefinite character, indifferent to the nauseous atmosphere that prevails in this somber tale; the recitative is solemn but restrained; and, as in *The Betrayal*, the tone established by the Latin language, stamped with an epic sobriety, predominates over the more French tone that would increasingly inform everything that

---

5. "Les Oratorios de Marc-Antoine Charpentier," *Recherches dans la musique classique française*, III (1963), 91–130. Excerpts translated for this volume by the editor. (Shortly before his untimely death in early 1977, Professor Barber wrote: "I regret that I am at present unable to find the English original. . . . If there is any material in the article you wish to extract [with reverse translation] you certainly have my permission to do so. . . .")

Charpentier was to write later. Moreover, it will be noted that in both instances the work is continuous, not divided into independent movements. Their harmony, often chromatic, and their tonal language are quite indecisive—an ambiguity not dissipated even by the cadences, which are related rather to the more or less modal cadences of Carissimi than to the relatively "recent" II-V-I or IV-V-I types which were then in process of formation and which the use of the new harmonic language, soon to be a commonplace [in Charpentier's music], would soon establish firmly in the musical thought of the composer. Then again, let us note a musical symbol, borrowed from Monteverdi and the madrigalists of the previous century, which depicts the gasping of someone in distress: the rest that breaks up the word "sus . . . pirabunt" [*recte* "suspira . . . bant"]. Our hypothesis seems to be confirmed in general by a musical material lacking in development. One might insist that the very aim of the work was one requiring the composer to limit it quantitatively and to eliminate all non-essentials, in the name of unity, tightness, and bare-bones economy; perhaps so, but the Jesuits of rue Saint-Antoine would never demand such restraint. Then too, how can we explain that the entire first part of the work is in rondo form, with the same musical material appearing three times with different combinations of performers, to it being added a modest ritornel for the flutes that appears twice (contributing nothing to the piece, in either a formal or an expressive way)? Let us conclude that *The Plague* is a youthful work—at least until more information [about it] is forthcoming.

Howard E. Smither
[*from "Marc-Antoine Charpentier and the Latin Oratorio"*][6]

Howard E. Smither, Professor of Music at The University of North Carolina, is a recent contributor to the literature on Charpentier's oratorios, in one chapter of his monumental three-volume history of the genre. We reprint those portions of his essay on Charpentier that are most relevant to Pestis Mediolanensis.

. . . Like the Latin works of Carissimi, those of Charpentier raise some difficult questions of terminology and classification. Charpentier designated none of his works by the term *oratorio*, and in fact that term was virtually never used in seventeenth-century France.[7] One might expect Claude François Ménestrier, in his book entitled *Des Représentations en musique anciennes et modernes* (Paris, 1681), to have used the term in his discussion of the oratorios sponsored by the Oratorians of Rome, but instead he speaks only of *musique dramatique*, as he does in his references to the sacred dramatic works of Charpentier.[8] Among Charpentier's designations for his works that are similar in varying degrees to the genre commonly identified by the term *oratorio* in Italy are *motet, canticum, historia, dialogus,* and *méditation*. Some of his works of this type bear no designation of a genre but only titles and/or indications of the feasts of the church calendar for which they are appropriate. Nevertheless, since a number of Charpentier's Latin works are like oratorios and since they clearly derive from Italy—in particular from Carissimi—it seems reasonable to apply the Italian term *oratorio* to them and to assess their historical position at least partially in terms of Italian music. . . .

. . . [Charpentier's oratorios] do not reflect the normal operatic conception of the oratorio of their own period, as exemplified in the oratorios of such

6. *A History of the Oratorio* (Chapel Hill: The University of North Carolina Press, 1977), I:419–32.

7. For a discussion of the rare use of the term *oratorio* in France, see Howard E. Smither, "Carissimi's Latin Oratorios: Their Terminology, Functions, and Position in Oratorio History," *Studien zur italienisch-deutschen Musikgeschichte, Analecta musicologica* 11 (1976): 53–78. (This and the following footnotes are Professor Smither's. I have renumbered them for the present volume and have given full bibliographical data for items abbreviated in Professor Smither's notes.)

8. [Claude François Ménestrier], *Des Représentations en musique anciennes et modernes* (Paris: René Guignard, 1681), pp. 191–92.

composers as Legrenzi, Stradella, Colonna, and A. Scarlatti (whose early period coincides with that of the works in the above list); rather, these works by Charpentier are closer in general conception (although not in the details of musical style) to the mid-century Latin oratorios of Carissimi, D. Mazzocchi, Marazzoli, F. Foggia, and Graziani. Thus the most appropriate frame of reference for understanding many of the features of [them] is that of the Latin oratorio of mid-century Rome, and it is in the mid-century Roman sense that the present author applies the term *oratorio* to them.

Few specifics are known about the exact places and dates of the performances of Charpentier's oratorios. Although they may have been performed at Lenten concerts in churches, there is evidence that they functioned at times as motets in a liturgical context[9]—as some of Carissimi's Latin oratorios may well have done. Charpentier's *Judicium Salomonis*, a work of about thirty-five minutes in length, for example, was performed as a motet at a mass celebrated for a special event. The work entitled simply *Elevation*, with a text on the subject of the Eucharist, was clearly intended to be performed during the canon of a mass. The Christmas oratorios . . . have texts closely related to the Gospel for midnight mass. In fact, all but three of Charpentier's oratorios are settings of texts appropriate for certain feast days; the exceptions are [*Mors*] *Saulis et Jonathae, Dialogus inter Christum et peccatores*, and *Josue*.

The texts of Charpentier's oratorios,[10] all anonymous, are similar to those of Carissimi's in several respects: most are based on biblical stories; the techniques of elaborating the biblical material are similar; and the nonbiblical insertions, largely in prose, employ similar rhetorical devices through which the prose at times approaches the condition of poetry. Among the texts based on the Bible, three use the same subjects as Carissimi's oratorios; these three are *Extremum Dei Judicium, Sacrificium Abrahae*, and *Judicium Salomonis*. Among the oratorios based on biblical stories that frequently served as the bases of oratorios throughout the Baroque era are *Judith, Historia Esther, Filius prodigus, Mors Saulis et Jonathae*, and *Josue*. Representing the hagiographical oratorio are three works based on the life of St. Cecilia. . . . In the biblical oratorios the Vulgate text is seldom quoted verbatim but is elaborated in a variety of ways: modified word order, paraphrase in prose, and nonbiblical insertions in prose and occasionally in poetry. The two biblical texts that are closest to the Vulgate are *Judith* and *Esther*; characteristic of those that use the biblical material only as a skeleton for the drama are *Filius prodigus, Extremum Dei Judicium*, and *Caedes sanctorum innocentium*.

If Charpentier's oratorios are conservative and reflect the mid-century in their general conception, they are by no means so in their musical style. While in some respects they reveal Carissimi's stylistic influence, it is blended with Italian and French styles characteristic of Charpentier's own generation. The recitatives occasionally employ the triadic and sequential melodic patterns prominent in Carissimi's music, but they share with Lully's recitatives their tendency to include a greater variety of note values, a wider range of pitch, and a greater number of large intervals than do the recitatives of either Carissimi or later seventeenth-century Italians. The general tendency in the second half of the seventeenth century to intermingle sections in recitative, arioso, and aria styles is present in Charpentier's oratorios, both within passages that are primarily recitative and within arias. . . .

. . . In Charpentier's oratorios the chorus is used far more than in contemporary Italian oratorios. At times the chorus functions in the role of the narrator, or *historicus*, although that role is also given to soloists and ensembles as it is in Carissimi's oratorios. Other functions of the chorus are to represent a crowd within the drama, to comment on the action, or to present a concluding, moralistic summary. In the shorter works these functions tend to be taken over by ensembles of soloists. While the choruses in Charpentier's oratorios are comparable to those in Carissimi's in regard to their extent and function, they are not comparable in style, for Charpentier's choruses are clearly products of their own time: in their harmonic resources and concertato combinations with instruments, they reflect the influence of the French *grand motet* of

---

9. For discussion of the functions of Charpentier's oratorios, see H. Wiley Hitchcock, "The Latin Oratorios of Marc-Antoine Charpentier" (Ph.D. dissertation, University of Michigan, 1954), I: 99–108, and Hitchcock, "The Latin Oratorios of Marc-Antoine Charpentier," *The Musical Quarterly* 41 (1955): 45–46.

10. All the texts, together with some music examples, are given in Hitchcock, "The Latin Oratorios" (diss.), vol. 2.

the second half of the seventeenth century. Although in Carissimi's oratorios chordal style prevails, in those of Charpentier it is balanced by counterpoint, usually imitative, that is more intricate than that of most Italian or French choral music in Charpentier's own time. Among the other choral resources of these oratorios are polychoral antiphony and the alternation of choral passages with those of soloists, small vocal ensembles, or instrumental groups, such as a trio of two woodwinds and continuo.

A feature of Charpentier's oratorios that is unusual in comparison with either Carissimi's or with those of composers in Charpentier's own generation is the emphasis upon instrumental music. Even in the shorter works the instruments, usually a trio-sonata ensemble of two violins and continuo, tend to be used more than in most seventeenth-century oratorios. In some of the works, an orchestra of four strings is used in addition to the trio-sonata group; three of the oratorios . . . call for a double orchestra of two string sections with four parts each. To the strings are sometimes added pairs of flutes, oboes, bassoons, and trumpets.[11] The instrumental music of the oratorios consists not only of ritornellos and accompaniment for the voices, but it also includes some remarkable programmatic numbers —"'night symphonies', 'awakening symphonies', 'enchantment symphonies', fanfares, marches, and *bruits de guerre*."[12]

11. For a tabular summary of the instrumentation, see Hitchcock, "The Latin Oratorios" (diss.), I: 312.
12. Hitchcock, "The Latin Oratorios" (art.), p. 55.

Index

A
Assoucy, Charles d'. *See* Dassoucy

B
Ballard (publishers), 4
Barber, Clarence H., 68
Basse continue. *See* Basso continuo
Basso continuo, 6, 7, 9, 11, 65, 71
Bassoon, 9, 11, 71
Berretta, Francesco, 3
Bobillier, Marie. *See* Brenet
Bordes, Charles, 12, 66
Borromeo, Charles, 5, 6, 7, 13, 14, 68
Brenet, Michel, 66
Brossard, Sébastien de, 3, 4, 65, 66

C
Canticum, 5, 6, 68, 69
Carissimi, Giacomo, 3, 5, 6, 7, 64, 66, 67, 68, 69, 70, 71
Cello, 8, 9
Chaperon, François, 4
Chartres, Philippe, Duc de, 3, 66
Chorus, 5, 7, 9, 11, 67, 70, 71
Clefs, 8
Colonna, Giovanni Paolo, 70
Comédie-Française. *See* Molière
Congregazione dell'Oratorio. *See* Oratorio, Congregazione dell'
Continuo, basso. *See* Basso continuo
Contralto, 11
Corneille, Thomas, 4
Croches blanches, 8, 11

D
Dassoucy, Charles, 3
Dauphin, the Grand (Monseigneur), 3, 67
De Brossard. *See* Brossard
De Guise, Duchesse (Marie de Lorraine), 3, 4, 68
Dessus, 8, 11
Dialogue. See *Dialogus*
Dialogus, 5, 66, 67, 68, 69
Doubling, 8, 9
Du Tillet. *See* Titon du Tillet

E
Edouard, Jacques, 4

F
Flute (*flûte*), 6, 8, 9, 11, 69, 71
Foggia, Francesco, 70

G
Grand motet. *See* Motet
Graziani, Bonifazio, 70
Guise, de. *See* De Guise

H
Haute-contre, 4, 8, 11, 67
Hemiola, 11
Histoire sacrée, 5, 12, 66, 67
Historia, 5, 68, 69
Historicus, 5, 67, 70
Holy Cross, Archconfraternity of the, 64

J
Jesuits, 4, 66, 67, 68, 69

L
Le Cerf de la Viéville, Jean Laurent, 4
Legrenzi, Giovanni, 70
Lochon, Jacques François, 65
Lorraine, Marie de. *See* De Guise
Louis XIV, 3, 67, 68
Lully, Jean-Baptiste, 3, 4, 66, 67, 68, 70

M
Marazzoli, Marco, 70
Marie-Thérèse (Queen), 67
Maugars, André, 64
Mazzochi, Domenico, 70
"Mélanges autographes," 4, 5, 67
Mercure galant, 3
Messe rouge, 4, 70
Milan, 6, 13, 68
Molière (Jean-Baptiste Poquelin), 3, 4, 6, 66
Monseigneur (Grand Dauphin). *See* Dauphin
Monteverdi, Claudio, 7, 69
Motet, 4, 5, 6, 9, 11, 12, 65, 66, 67, 68, 69; *grand motet*, 67, 70

N
Narrator. See *Historicus*
Neri, St. Philip, 6

O
Oboe, 9, 71
Opéra, 4, 67
Oratorians. *See* Oratorio, Congregazione dell'
Oratorio, 4, 5, 6, 64, 65, 66, 67, 68, 69, 70, 71
Oratorio, Congregazione dell', 6, 69

Organ, 11, 64
Orléans, Duke of. *See* Chartres
Ornaments, 11

P
Paris, 3, 4, 6, 64
Philippe, Duc de Chartres. *See* Chartres
Plague (Milan, 1576–77), 5, 6, 7, 13, 68
Prelude, 5, 6, 7, 8, 68

Q
Quinte, 8

R
Recitative, 7, 64, 70
Recorder. *See* Flute
Ritornel, 6, 7, 9, 11, 65, 69, 71
Rome, 3, 64, 65
Rondeau, 6, 7, 69
Rondo. See *Rondeau*

S
Sainte-Chapelle, 3, 4, 64, 68
Saint-Louis (church), 4
San Marcello, 64
Santissimo Crocifisso. *See* Holy Cross
Scarlatti, Alessandro, 70
Schola Cantorum (Paris), 12, 66
Smither, Howard E., 69
Stradella, Alessandro, 70
Sun King. *See* Louis XIV

T
Taille, 8
Tenor, 11
Tillet. *See* Titon du Tillet
Titon du Tillet, 3
Transposition, 6n, 12

V
Versailles, 4
Violin, 8, 11, 65, 71
Violon, basse de, 8, 9
Violoncello. *See* Cello
Viols, 8

W
Waldman, Frederic, 12

THE AUTHOR

H. Wiley Hitchcock, *professor of music and director of
the Institute for Studies in American Music at Brooklyn College,
is the author of a number of books, among them*
Music in the United States: A Historical Introduction *and* Ives;
*he is also series editor for several textbook
and research publications in musicology.*

A NOTE ON THE BOOK

*Text set in Photocomposition Palatino
Composition by The University of North Carolina Press*

*Printed on sixty-pound Olde Style by
S. D. Warren Company, Boston, Massachusetts*

*Cover stock, seventy-pound Corsican, by
Simpson Paper Company, Vicksburg, Michigan*

*Cloth spine, Roxite B 51565, by
Holliston Mills, Inc., Norwood, Massachusetts*

*Printing and binding by
Kingsport Press, Kingsport, Tennessee*

*Designed and published by
The University of North Carolina Press*

Sale
$ ~~2.00~~
051842

1.00
010795